PICTURE DICTIONARY

Cover and interior illustration by Michele Nidenoff

Copyright © 1997 Modern Publishing, a division of Unisystems, Inc.
® Honey Bear Books is a trademark owned by Honey Bear Productions, Inc.,
and is registered in the U.S. Patent and Trademark Office.
No part of this book may be reproduced or copied in any form without written permission from the publisher.

© 1997 Fisher-Price, Inc. Fisher-Price trademarks are used under license from Fisher-Price, Inc.
Character designs are trademarks of Fisher-Price, Inc.
Manufactured for and distributed by Modern Publishing, a division of Unisystems, Inc. New York, New York 10022

Modern Publishing
A Division of Unisystems, Inc.
New York, New York 10022
Printed in the U.S.A.

CAN YOU FIND THESE WORDS PICTURED?

acorn

alphabet block

airplane

apple

alligator

artist

acorn — An acorn seed falls from the tree.

animal — My pets are animals.

alphabet — A is the first letter of the alphabet. Do you know the other letters?

answer — Do you know the answer to the question?

ambulance — The ambulance is an automobile that brings sick people to the hospital.

ant — The ant is a very small insect.

ape — The hairy ape loves to eat bananas.

arms — I have two arms on my body.

apple — Apples are red and juicy fruit that grow on trees.

arrow — The sharp arrow was shot into the target. Bullseye!

apron — An apron helps keep dad's shirt clean while he cooks.

ate — I ate an apple. Yum!

CAN YOU FIND THESE WORDS PICTURED?

baby   beads   book
ball   bed   boy
bandage   bedroom   brown
banner   blocks   building
basket   blue
bat   boat

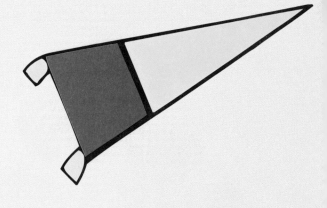

bath — When I am dirty, I wash myself in the bath.

bear — The bear is a big, furry animal. Grrr!

beach — It is fun to play in the sand and water at the beach.

bed — I sleep in my bed at night.

beads — The beads fit together to make a pretty necklace.

bee — The buzzing bee flies from flower to flower.

boots — Boots keep your feet warm and dry.

brush — My hair looks nice and neat when I use a brush.

bread — A sandwich has two slices of bread.

bus — I ride a bus to school.

bridge — The cars drive over the bridge to get across the water.

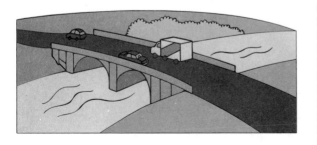

button — The round button keeps my coat closed.

C c

CAN YOU FIND THESE WORDS PICTURED?

camera	caterpillar	cow
car	claw	crab
carrot	cloud	crawl
cat	clown	cuff

cat — My pet cat says, "Meow."

chicken — The chicken is a bird that does not fly.

catch — Throw me the ball and I will catch it.

clap — Put your hands together to clap for the actors.

chair — Everyone sits in a chair at the table.

climb — You can climb up to the top of the castle.

color — Can you name the colors of the rainbow?

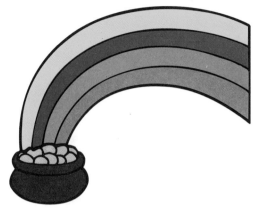

cow — The cow is an animal that gives milk. Moo!

comb — I comb my hair to get out the knots.

crayon — I color in a picture with a wax crayon.

cook — I help mom cook dinner on the stove in the kitchen.

cup — We drink juice out of a cup.

Dd

CAN YOU FIND THESE WORDS PICTURED?

dad   dog house
daisy   door
dish   drinks
dog   driving

dad — My dad keeps me safe and gives me lots of love. He is a good father.

deep — The ocean is deep. It is a long way from top to bottom.

dark — Let's shine the flashlight so that we can see in the dark.

desk — I sit in a chair at my desk to do my homework.

day — Every morning is the start of a new day.

dig — My dog likes to dig holes in the dirt to bury his bones.

down — Whee! Watch me slip down the slide.

draw — Let's draw a picture with my crayons.

doze — I like to doze in my sleeping bag.

drum — Rat-a-tat-tat! Listen to me beat music on the drum.

dragon — The knight fights the fire-breathing dragon.

Ee

CAN YOU FIND THESE WORDS PICTURED?

ears
edge
eggs
electrical outlet

elephant
empty
eyes

earn — I earn money when I walk my neighbor's dog. She pays me twenty-five cents.

eat — I eat three meals every day. Mommy says to chew before I swallow.

ears — Your ears help you to hear sounds.

edge — I walk up to the pool. Then I sit at the edge and wait for my teacher.

easy — It is easy to fit this simple puzzle together.

egg — The baby chick hatches from the egg.

elephant — Cindy rides the big, gray elephant at the zoo.

empty — When Maya finishes eating, her bowl is empty. There is nothing left.

explore — My sister and I like to explore. We found a ladybug. Look!

end — One end of the string has a knot. I can slide beads on at the other end.

eyes — Your eyes help you see colors and shapes.

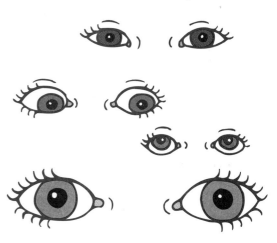

F f

CAN YOU FIND THESE WORDS PICTURED?

face
fan
feather
feed
feet
fingers

fish
flashlight
floor
flower
food

face — Your face has two eyes, a nose, and a mouth.

fast — Billy likes to run fast. He wins many races.

fall — Leaves fall from treetops to the ground.

fat — The circus elephant is big and fat.

farm — The farmer plants crops to grow food on the farm.

feathers — The soft feathers on a bird help it to fly.

24

feed — I feed the birds with seeds all winter long.

find — Look in the attic and find some old clothes to wear.

feels — I hug kitty. She feels soft.

fingers — You have five fingers on each hand.

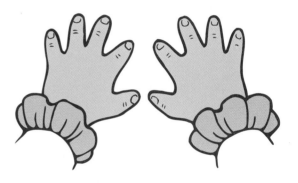

feet — You have ten toes on your feet. Let's count them!

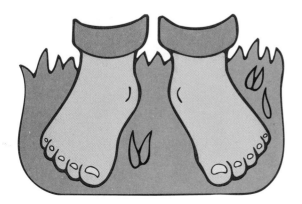

first — The boy is first in line. The girls are behind him.

fish — There are many colorful fish in the sea.

flat — The desert road is flat. There are no bumps or dips.

flowers — The flowers in the meadow are beautiful.

flip — Flip the pancake over so that it does not burn.

food — You eat food to stay strong and healthy.

forest — Walk through the forest to see the trees, birds, and animals.

friends — Tasha and Wanda are friends. They like each other.

four — Three is the number before four. How many trikes do you count?

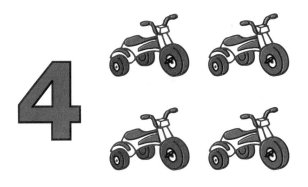

frogs — A frog is a small green animal that hops around and says "ribbit."

fresh — Vegetables just picked from the garden are fresh. They are juicy and taste good.

fun — Kathy has fun playing with the sprinkler. It makes her happy.

G g

CAN YOU FIND THESE WORDS PICTURED?

garden grandma green
gate grandpa ground
ghost grapes growing
girl grass
goat gray

GARDEN

game — I play a game for fun.

gate — Close the gate so that the baby can't get out.

ghost — A scary ghost is in the haunted house.

giant — A great, big giant chased Jack down the beanstalk.

gift — The best present is a gift that comes from the heart.

giggle — We like to giggle and laugh at funny jokes.

glum — The frowning clown looks sad. He is glum.

girl — When a little girl grows up, she becomes a woman.

go — Watch the train go around the track. It moves.

glad — The laughing clown looks glad. He is happy.

good — The hero is good and nice. The villain is bad and mean.

goose — The honking goose flew south for the winter.

grapes — Round, juicy grapes are fruit that grow in bunches on vines.

grab — I grab hold of my daddy's hand before crossing the street.

grass — The green grass makes a beautiful lawn.

grade — I study hard to earn a good grade on tests at school.

green — What else is the color green besides grass?

greet — Friends greet each other with a handshake.

grin — The joke was so funny that I had to smile and grin.

grill — Dad cooks hamburgers on the grill.

gruff — The gruff bulldog is rough and tough.

gum — I like to chew peppermint gum.

H h

CAN YOU FIND THESE WORDS PICTURED?

hang	hill
hat	hole
helicopter	horse
hello	hot
hen	house
hike	husband

hair — Mom braids my hair in a ponytail.

hang — Please hang your clothes up in the closet.

hall — The hall leads from the front door to the living room.

happy — The happy clown laughed.

ham — I like to eat ham sandwiches for lunch.

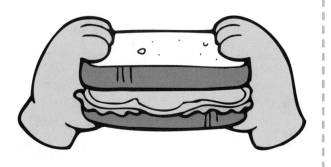

hat — The actress wears a feathered hat on her head. How many hats can you name?

heel — My sock fits over my heel at the back of my foot.

help — Will you help your brother with the household chores?

hem — Mom hems my dress to make it shorter.

hello — Do you say hello when you answer the telephone?

hen — The clucking hen lays eggs in her nest.

hide — Pirates hide treasure so that no one can find it.

hiss — A snake hiss means danger!

hike — I hike on the nature trail carrying my knapsack.

hit — I hit the baseball with a bat.

hill — The hill is at the foot of the mountain.

hog — The hog lives in a muddy pig-pen.

hole — A rabbit lives in a hole in the ground.

hot — We need an umbrella to shade us from the hot sun.

home — Mommy and Daddy make our house a loving home.

hug — I hug my cuddly dog with both arms.

hop — I hop up and down on a pogo-stick.

huge — The elephant is huge. The mouse is small.

CAN YOU FIND THESE WORDS PICTURED?

ice   insect
idea   invite
in   ivy

ice — Tea tastes good and cold with ice cubes.

imagine — Can you imagine the job you will have when you are a grown-up? Think about it.

idea — I thought of an idea for a new invention.

important — It is important to see a doctor if you are sick. It matters very much.

igloo — In the past, some Eskimos made igloo houses out of blocks of ice.

inch — Twelve inches make one foot.

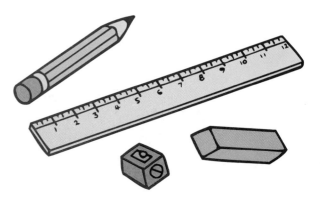

ink — This pen is out of ink. I can't write.

inside — Do you stay inside your house when it rains outside?

insect — A mosquito is a flying insect. Can you name the other bugs?

invite — Will you invite your friends to your birthday party?

iron — A hot iron smooths wrinkled clothes.

J j

CAN YOU FIND THESE WORDS PICTURED?

jacket	jester
jack-in-the-box	jet
jack-o-lantern	jolly
jar	jug
jelly	jump

jacket — Don't forget to wear a warm jacket when the weather is cold.

jet — The jet airplane flew over my house.

jam — I like to eat strawberry jam on my toast.

job — My job is hard work.

jar — The lid on the jelly jar is hard to open.

jog — We jog around the park in our running shorts.

joy — The batter hit a home run. The crowd jumped with joy. Hooray!

jug — This jug has apple cider in it. That jug holds water.

June — June is the month before July.

jump — Jill and Jane hop, skip, and jump rope.

junk — The junk yard is full of broken and useless things.

K k

CAN YOU FIND THESE WORDS PICTURED?

key   kite
kick   kitten
kid   knock
kiss

kangaroo — The young kangaroo hops in and out of its mother's pouch.

kick — Soccer is a game in which you kick a ball.

kettle — I put water in the kettle to boil for tea.

kid — A kid is a baby goat. Sometimes a child is called a kid. It's true. I wouldn't kid you!

key — Only one key fits the lock that will open the door.

kind — The boy treats his baby sister very well. He is nice and kind to her.

kitchen —The kitchen is the room in which we cook.

knife — Mom uses a sharp knife to cut the tomato.

kite — It's fun to fly a kite in the spring. Watch it sail in the air!

knight — A knight protects the castle.

kitten — A kitten is a baby cat. Meow!

know — Do you know how to add numbers? Do you understand what to do?

L l

CAN YOU FIND THESE WORDS PICTURED?

ladder	lawn	lift
lake	leaf	little
large	leap	loon
laugh	left	lunch

ladder — Climb up the ladder to reach the apples.

last — The last girl is at the end of the line.

lake — A lake is a body of water with land around it.

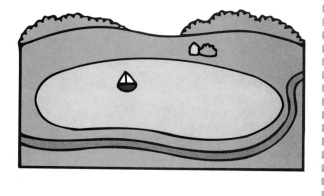

late — Dad was in a hurry and late for his meeting. He did not make it in time.

large — A whale is large. It is a big animal.

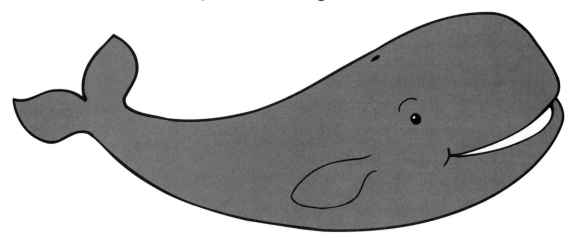

lazy — A lazy worker does not do his work.

left — This arrow is pointing to the left.

leap — The kids play leap frog. They have fun jumping over one another.

less — The number 3 is less than 6.

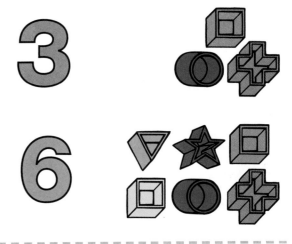

learn — After I learn how to take care of my puppy I will know what to do.

let — Will mom let you go to the store? Will she allow you to do it?

letter — Grandma sent you a letter. Let's read what she wrote.

lift — Two people need to lift and carry the sofa to the truck.

light — Turn the light on, please. Then we can see.

like — Which toy do you like the best? Which one will you choose?

lion — The lion roars. Have you seen this animal in a zoo?

long — Tom has one long sock and one short sock.

love — Grandpa always says, "I love you," and gives me a kiss. He cares about me.

lost — Our puppy was lost. Then we found her behind a bush.

low — It is a low fence. It is not very tall.

loud — The taxi driver honked his horn. It made a loud sound.

lunch — Lunch time comes between breakfast and dinner.

Mm

CAN YOU FIND THESE WORDS PICTURED?

magic
man
marionette
marker
mask

merry-go-round
money
mother
music

mail — People mail letters to one another.

mask — Boo! I made a mask with a paper bag.

map — My map shows how to get from one place to another.

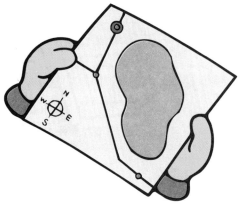

mat — A mat is a small rug.

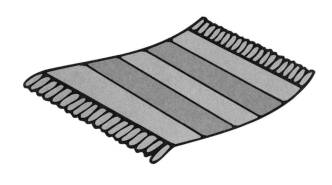

marker — Use a red marker to draw a picture of an apple.

match — Can you match these shoes and boots? Which ones go together?

meet — I meet friends on the playground. We talk and play together.

middle — The hen is in the middle.

merry-go-round — The horses on a merry-go-round go up and down and round and round.

milk — Milk is a drink that comes from cows. Do you put milk on your cereal?

mess — This room is a mess. It is time to clean up and put the toys away.

mind — Jose will mind the baby. He will watch and take good care of her.

mine — This dress is mine. It belongs to me.

monkey — The monkey swings in trees. Have you seen a monkey at the zoo?

mix — Mix the flour with the eggs and butter in a bowl.

month — May is one month. Can you name the other eleven?

money — You need money to buy the things you want or need.

moon — You can see the moon in the night sky. The moon moves around the earth once every month.

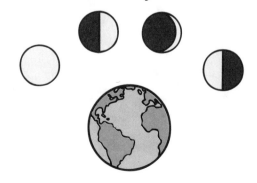

mop — We use a mop to wash the floor.

move — Push the broken car to move it from one place to another.

morning — I get up in the morning when the sun comes up.

mud — Mud is wet dirt. Do you ever make squishy mud pies?

mother — My mother is a loving parent. She takes care of me and my brother.

music — You can listen and dance to music. You can sing along too.

N n

CAN YOU FIND THESE WORDS PICTURED?

nail   neighbor   nine

nap   nest   noise

necklace   newspaper   nurse

nail — Ruth hit the nail into the wood with a hammer.

near — My house is not far from school. I live near school. It is close.

name — My name, Susie, is on my T-shirt. What's your name?

neck — The giraffe has a long neck.

nap — The sleepy baby takes a nap in the afternoon.

need — People must have water to live. People need water to live.

needle — Grandma uses a sharp needle and thread to sew clothes.

nest — Some birds live in a nest.

neighbor — Sonya and Ed live near each other. Sonya is Ed's neighbor.

net — A large net is used to catch fish in the ocean.

newspaper — You can read the news in the newspaper. You can learn what's happening in your town, country, and the world.

nickel — A nickel is a coin that is worth five cents.

nod — You can nod your head up and down.

night — You can see the stars and moon at night.

noise — The loud noise kept me awake.

nine — Nine is a number. Nine is one more than eight.

nose — I use my nose to breath and smell.

number — 1, 2, 3, 4, 5, 6, 7, 8, 9, and 10 are numbers. Which number tells how old you are?

note — A note is a short, written message.

nurse — A nurse is a person who helps care for sick people.

nothing — An empty carton has nothing in it.

nut — A nut is a seed that has a hard shell.

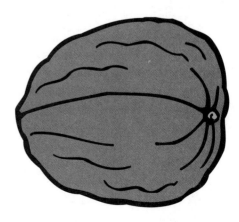

O o

CAN YOU FIND THESE WORDS PICTURED?

ocean	one
October	open
octopus	orange
office	outside
old	

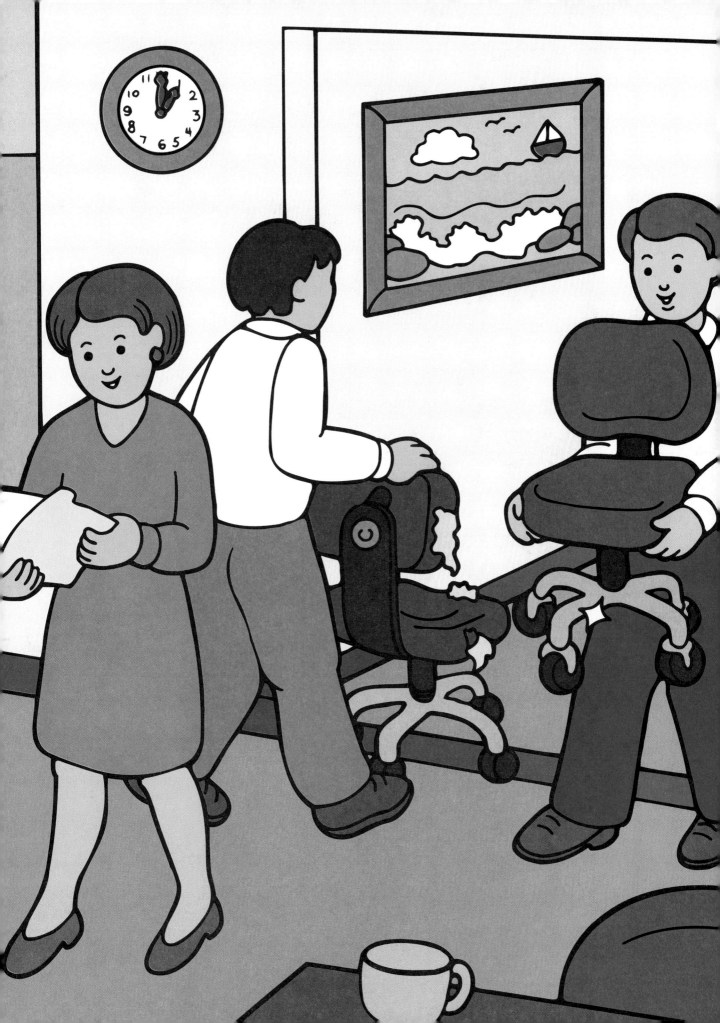

ocean — An ocean is a large body of salt water.

o'clock — I eat breakfast at 8 o'clock in the morning.

off — Take off your wet boots when you come into the house.

octopus — An octopus is a sea animal with 8 arms.

offer — I ask Dad if he needs help. I offer to help.

office — Some people work in an office at a desk.

once — Darryl read the book only one time. Darryl read the book once.

often — Something that happens often happens again and again. It often snows in January.

one — One is a number. Mom says that I can have only one cupcake.

old — This is an old frame. It has been in the family for a long time.

onion — An onion is a vegetable. It is round and grows underground.

open — If you open the box you can see what is inside.

order — The children put the alphabet blocks in the correct order.

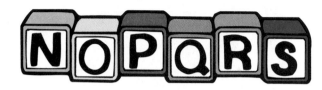

orange — Orange is a color. A pumpkin is orange.

ostrich — An ostrich is a big bird that cannot fly.

orchestra — We listened to the orchestra play music.

other — I have two hands. One is my right hand. The other is my left hand.

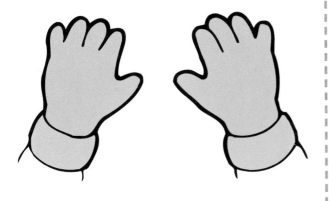

oven — I bake the cake in a hot oven.

our — These toys belong to us. They are our toys.

owl — An owl is a bird that is awake at night.

out — When we get to school we get out of the school bus.

own — This roadster is mine. I own it. It belongs to me.

P p

CAN YOU FIND THESE WORDS PICTURED?

paint   pencil   plant
palace   pet   pretty
paper   picture   princess
pen   pink   puzzle

pages — You go from page to page when you read a storybook.

pail — I carry water and sand in a pail.

palace — The prince and princess live in a royal palace.

pajamas — Pajamas are clothes that you wear when you go to bed.

pan — Dad cooked the eggs in a pan on the stove.

paper — Here is some paper for you to write on.

parrot — A parrot is a bird with bright, colored feathers.

parent — My mother and father are my parents.

pay — Dad will pay for the groceries. He will give money to the clerk.

park — I play on the grass and trees at the park.

peanut — Take the shell off the peanut before you eat it.

pick — Choose one fruit. Which one did you pick?

picture — The girl painted a picture of a toy.

picnic — We eat our picnic lunch outside.

pie — A pie may be filled with fruit. It is baked in an oven.

piece — Each piece fits into the puzzle book.

pig — A pig is a short, fat animal with a flat nose. Oink!

plant — A plant is a living thing that is not a person or an animal.

pilot — A pilot is someone who flies an airplane.

play — The boys like to play a game of hockey. It is fun to play.

pirate — Someone who attacks and robs ships is a pirate.

police officer — A police officer's job is to protect everyone.

Q q

CAN YOU FIND THESE WORDS PICTURED?

quack   queen
quart   question
quarter   quilt

quack — "Quack! Quack!" said the duck.

queen — A queen is a woman who rules a country.

quart — Four cups make a quart. Four quarts make a gallon.

queer — I think it is queer that the puzzle pieces don't fit together. It is strange.

quarter — A quarter is a coin that equals twenty-five cents. Four quarters equal one dollar.

question — If you don't know something, ask a question to get the answer.

quick — A rabbit runs fast. A rabbit is a quick animal.

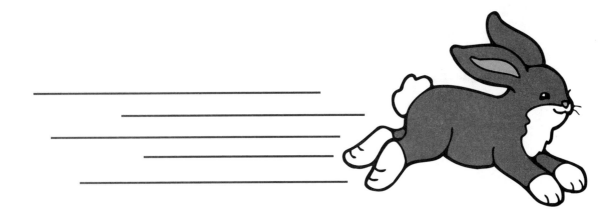

_____
_____
_____
_____
_____

quiet — Please do not make any noise. Please be quiet.

quit — He did not want to play any more. He quit playing the game.

quilt — A quilt is a stuffed blanket. The baby plays on the colorful quilt.

quite — Quite means very. It was quite cold after it snowed. It was very cold.

R r

CAN YOU FIND THESE WORDS PICTURED?

radio   robot
rain   rolls
rainbow   rose
restaurant   round
rice

rabbit — The long-eared rabbit hopped on its back legs.

rain — Water that falls in drops from clouds in the sky is called rain.

raccoon — A raccoon is a small, furry animal with a striped tail and black mask.

rainbow — After it rains there are seven colors in a rainbow. Can you name them?

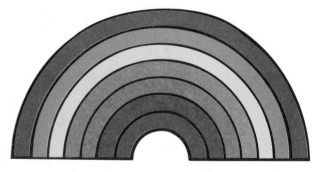

radio — We listen to music on the radio.

raincoat — Wear a raincoat to stay dry when you go out in the rain.

raise — Raise your hand so that I can see where you are. Lift up your hand.

read — Mommy reads the words in the book to me.

rake — A rake is a tool to gather leaves.

ready — I am all dressed and ready to go to school.

ranch — A ranch is a large farm where cows, horses, sheep, and pigs live.

ride — Do you ride to school or do you walk?

ring — I put the ring on my finger.

robot — A robot is a machine that works.

river — A large stream of water is a river.

rocket — The astronaut traveled through space in a rocket.

road — Cars and trucks travel on a road. It is a wide path.

roll — The puppy likes to turn over and over in the grass. The puppy likes to roll in the grass.

roof — The top of a building is called the roof. The roof of the doghouse is blue.

rope — You can tie things up with a rope.

room — The room in our house where we eat is the kitchen.

round — A ball is round like a circle.

rooster — A grown-up, male chicken is called a rooster. Cock-a-doodle-do!

rule — You must know every rule to play the game.

S s

CAN YOU FIND THESE WORDS PICTURED?

sad	ship	soap
sailboat	shirt	square
saw	shorts	star
school	sing	stool
scissors	sink	student
seven	sit	subtract
shape	six	sun
share	smile	

sad — The girl is sad because she cannot play outside. She is unhappy.

sand — We play in the sand at the beach.

sail — The pirates sail their ship on the ocean to an island.

sandwich — Put lettuce and cheese between two pieces of bread to make a sandwich.

same — The boy and girl both have blond hair. The color of their hair is the same.

save — I put money in the bank every week. I want to save enough money to buy new skates.

shark — A shark is a very big fish with sharp teeth.

sheep — A sheep is an animal covered with wool.

sing — The children make music with their voices. They sing a song.

ship — We sailed across the ocean on a ship.

sink — Wash your hands in the sink.

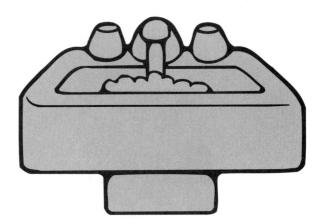

six — Six is a number. It is one more than five.

smile — I smile when I am happy.

sky — The sun is in the sky.

snow — When it is cold, snow falls from the clouds. It covers the ground like a white blanket.

sleep — When the baby gets tired, he goes to sleep.

soap — Wash your hands with soap to get the dirt off.

soft — The teddy bear feels soft and cuddly.

squirrel — A squirrel is a small, furry animal that lives in a tree and eats nuts.

spoon — I eat soup with a spoon.

store — I bought an apple at the store.

square — All four sides of a square are the same length. Can you name another shape?

sun — The sun shines brightly in the afternoon sky.

T t

CAN YOU FIND THESE WORDS PICTURED?

table	track
tail	train
teapot	tree
teddy bear	triangle
telephone pole	truck
ten	turtle
three	twelve
tire	two

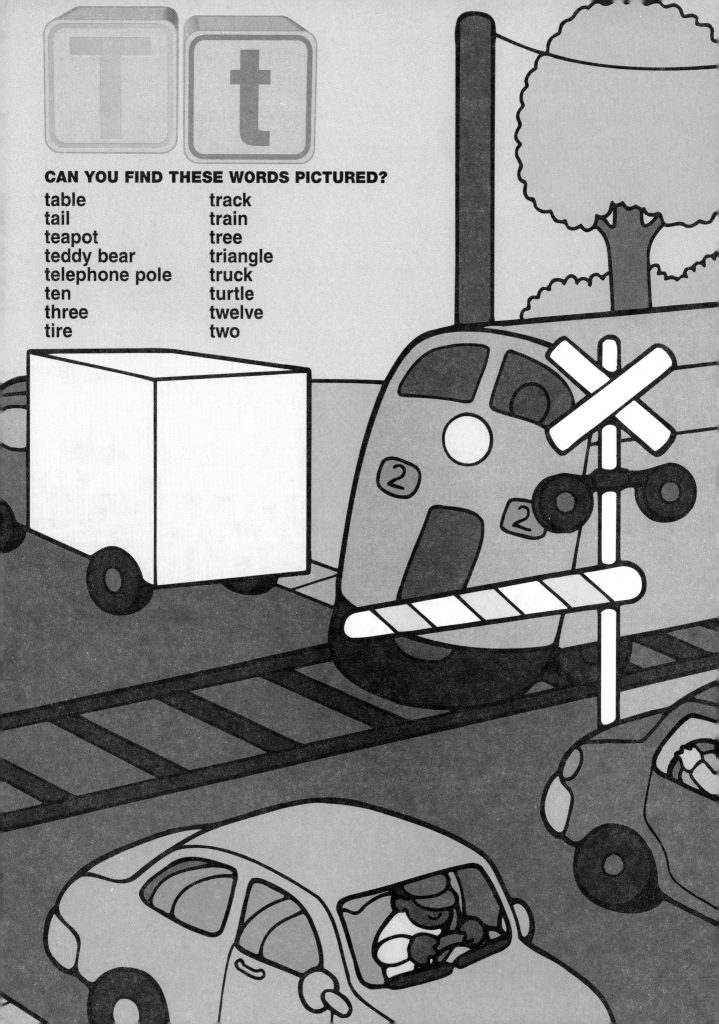

table — A table is a piece of furniture. It has a flat top and 4 legs.

tall — The tall tree grows far above the ground.

tail — A cat has a tail at the back of its body. What other animal has a tail?

teacher — A teacher helps you learn.

team —We are on the same soccer team. We play together against other teams.

teeth — Show your teeth when you smile.

tent — We slept in a tent when we went camping outdoors.

telephone — You can talk on the telephone with someone who lives far away.

thick — He cut a thick slice of bread.

ten — Ten is a number. It is one more than nine.

thin — She cut a thin slice of bread.

three — Three is a number. It is one more than two.

tomorrow — Today is April 1. We will go to the park tomorrow on April 2.

tiger — A tiger is an animal with orange fur and black stripes that lives in the jungle.

tower — Knights climb the high, castle tower.

tire — Dad had to fix a flat tire on the car.

track — The train runs on a track.

traffic — Many cars and trucks are on the road. There is a lot of traffic.

tree — Leaves fall from the tree.

turtle — A turtle can live on land or in the water. It has a hard shell.

truck — The truck carried our furniture to our new house.

two — Two is a number. It is one more than one.

U u

CAN YOU FIND THESE WORDS PICTURED?

ugly   unhappy
umbrella   up
under

ugly — The ugly house was not nice to look at.

under — The dog sleeps under the baby's bed.

umbrella — I use an umbrella to help me stay dry in the rain.

understand — I know how to use the camera. I understand how it works.

uncle — Your father's or mother's brother is your uncle.

UNCLE EARL

underwear — I put my underwear on first.

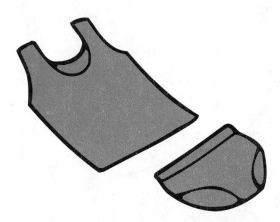

unhappy — We were unhappy that we couldn't see the movie. We were sad.

upstairs — I went upstairs to my bedroom.

up — The cat climbed up the tree.

use — We use scissors to cut paper. We use a crayon to draw. We use a fork to eat.

upside down — A ride on the roller coaster will turn you upside down.

V v

CAN YOU FIND THESE WORDS PICTURED?

vacuum   vegetable
valentine   vine
van   violin

vacuum — The vacuum cleaner picks up dirt around the house.

vegetable — A vegetable is a part of a plant that people eat. Corn is my favorite vegetable.

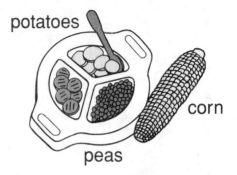

potatoes

corn

peas

valentine — I made a valentine for my sweetheart.

vest — He wore a vest over his shirt.

van — Our family likes to ride in a van.

vet — A vet is a doctor who takes care of animals.

village — A village is a small town.

vine — Pumpkins grow on a vine.

visit — We go to see my cousins. We visit my cousins.

violin — A violin is a musical instrument. To play it, you slide a bow over its strings.

voyage — A voyage is a trip by water. We took a voyage on a big ship.

Ww

CAN YOU FIND THESE WORDS PICTURED?

wag	water	woman
wagon	web	worm
walk	wet	
wash	white	

wags — My dog wags his tail when he is happy.

wash — We wash the car with soap and water until it is clean.

wagon — A wagon is used to carry things. It has four wheels and a handle.

watch — A watch is a small clock to wear on your wrist.

walk — We use our legs and feet to walk down the street.

water — Water is a clear liquid. We need to drink water to live.

weak — The man is weak. He cannot lift the heavy box. He is not strong.

week — Sunday, Monday, Tuesday, Wednesday, Thursday, Friday, and Saturday are the seven days of the week.

wear — I wear a hat on my head. I wear socks on my feet.

wet — If you go out in the rain, you will get wet.

web — A spider spins a web.

wheel — A wheel is round. Spinning wheels make our tricycles go.

wing — A bird has two wings to help it fly. How is an airplane like a bird?

whistle — Blow into the whistle to make a loud sound.

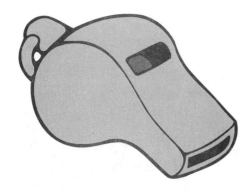

winter — Winter is a cold and snowy time of the year.

win — The person who finishes first will win the race.

wire — Electricity can move through a metal wire.

wolf — A wolf is an animal that looks like a wild dog.

woman — When a girl grows up, she becomes a woman.

world — Planet earth is our world. It is our home.

wood — Wood is used to make furniture, paper, and many other things.

worm — A worm is a small, skinny animal that lives in the ground.

X x

CAN YOU FIND THESE WORDS PICTURED?

x   xylophone

x-ray

X — X is the 24th letter of the alphabet. Point to the letter X.

EXIT EXTRA

x-ray — The doctor took an x-ray to see if I broke a bone.

x's and o's — When you play tic-tac-toe you use x's and o's.

Sometimes people put x's and o's on letters. The x's mean kisses. The o's mean hugs.

Dear Grandma-
How are you?
I am fine. See
you soon.
Love, Susie xoxo

x marks the spot — X marks the spot on a map to show where something is.

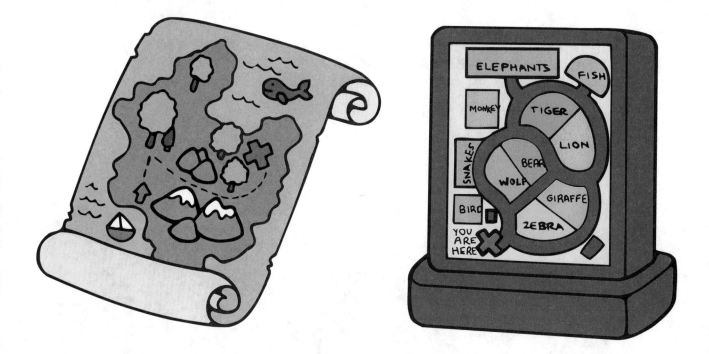

---

xylophone — A xylophone is a musical instrument. You hit metal rectangles with a small hammer to play the xylophone.

Y y

CAN YOU FIND THESE WORDS PICTURED?

yard   yellow
yarn   young
yell   yo-yo

yak — A yak is an animal with long hair that lives in the mountains.

yawn — I yawn when I am tired. I open my mouth and take a deep breath.

yard — You can play outside, but stay in the yard.

year — There are 12 months in one year.

1996

yarn — Yarn is used to make sweaters, socks, and scarves.

yell — Sometimes I yell to my dog to come home. I shout.

yellow — Yellow is a bright color. A banana is yellow. What other things are yellow?

young — A baby is a young child.

yet — We are not finished at this time. We are not finished yet.

yo-yo — I made the toy yo-yo go up and down by pulling its string.

you — When you look in a mirror, you see yourself!

Z z

CAN YOU FIND THESE WORDS PICTURED?

zebra   zoo
zero   zoom
zipper

$1.00

zebra — A zebra is an animal with black and white stripes that looks like a horse.

zipper — My jacket closes with a zipper instead of buttons.

zero — Zero is a number that means none or nothing. If you have zero in your basket, you have nothing in the basket.

zoo — We saw many animals at the zoo.

zip — Zip up your sweater before you go outside.

zoomed — The airplane zoomed into the sky.

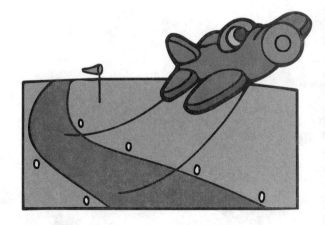